Contents

Words in **bold** are in the glossary.

The violin

A violin is a musical instrument with four strings. To make music with it, you stroke the strings with a bow or pluck them with your fingers.

A violin is made of wood. A bow is made of wood and horsehair.

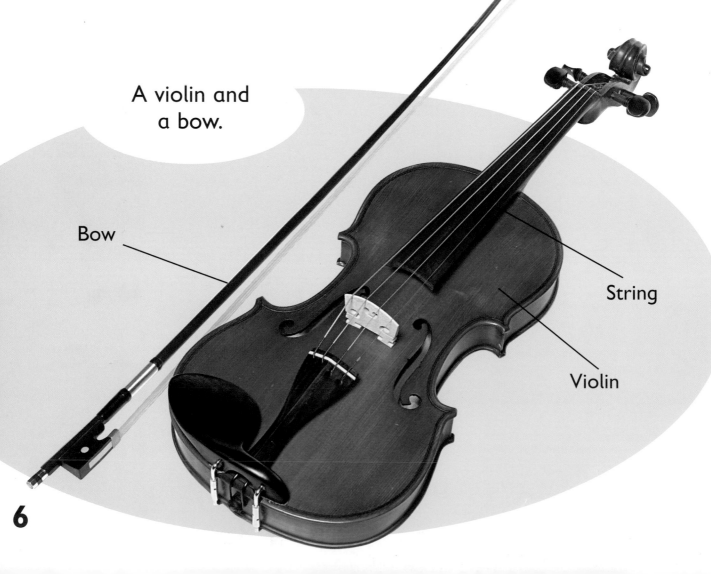

A violin and a bow.

Bow

String

Violin

Let's Make
MUSIC

Th
and
ins

FRANKLIN WATTS

First published in 2007 by
Franklin Watts
338 Euston Road
London NW1 3BH

Franklin Watts Australia
Level 17/207 Kent Street
Sydney NSW 2000

Art director: Jonathan Hair
Series designed and created for Franklin Watts by Painted Fish Ltd.
Designer: Rita Storey
Editor: Fiona Corbridge
Advisor: Helen MacGregor

Picture credits
istockphoto.com pp. 6, 9, 10, 11(bottom), 18, 19, 21–23, 25 and 26; Andrew
Lepley/Redferns p. 25; David Redfern/Redferns p. 22; Tudor Photography pp. 3, 7,
8, 11 (top), 12, 13, 14, 15, 16, 17, 20; Ulster Orchestra p. 24.

Cover images: Tudor Photography, Banbury (top); istock.com (bottom).

All photos posed by models.
Thanks to Husnen Ahmad, James Barlow, Maddi Indun, Mary Martin, Stephen
Morris, Jack Phillips, George Stapleton and Natasha Vinall.

ISBN 978 0 7496 7584 4

A CIP catalogue record for this book is available from the British Library.
Dewey Classification: 787

Printed in China

Franklin Watts is a division of Hachette Children's Books,
an Hachette Livre UK company.

How to play

To play a violin, tuck it between your chin and shoulder. Hold the bow in your other hand.

Making a sound

When you stroke the hair of the bow backwards and forwards against the strings of the violin, it makes sounds.

This boy is playing a violin with a bow.

Chin rest

Horsehair

Bow

Listen!
Page 28 tells you about music on stringed instruments that you can listen to.

The sound

When you play a string on a musical instrument, it wobbles very fast.
The string is vibrating.

Moving the air

When the string **vibrates**, it makes the air around it move as well. The way the air moves is called a **sound wave**.

Making waves

Stretch an elastic band over your fingers. Pull it gently and let go. Can you see it vibrate? The sound waves from the elastic band made the sound that you heard.

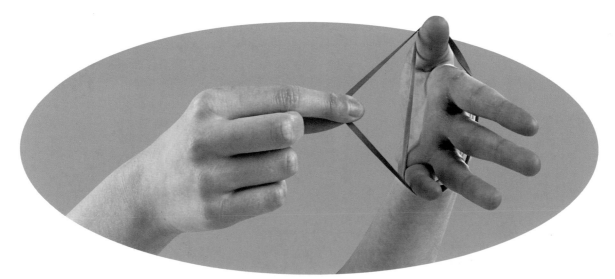

Getting louder

On a violin the strings are stretched across a piece of wood called a bridge.

When you play the strings, the **vibrations** go down the bridge into the hollow body of the violin. The sound gets louder and comes out through the sound holes.

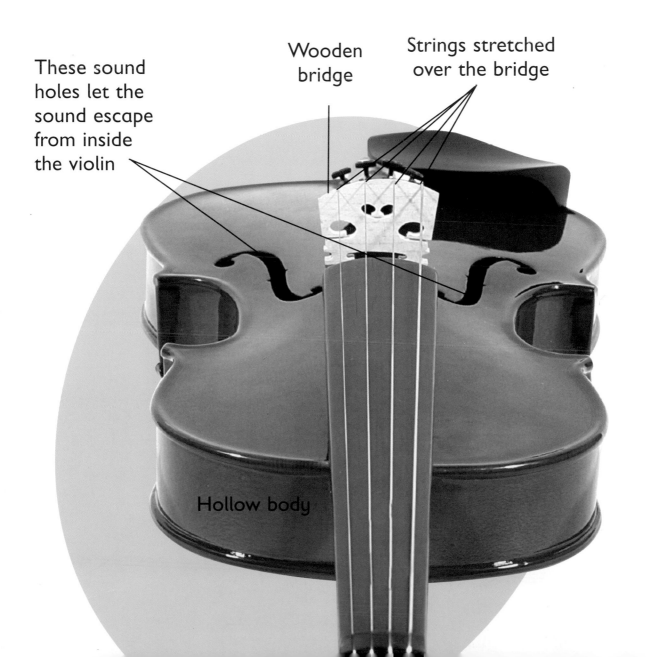

These sound holes let the sound escape from inside the violin

Wooden bridge

Strings stretched over the bridge

Hollow body

The strings

Each of the four strings on a violin makes a different sound, or musical note, when you play it.

These four notes on their own would not be enough to make interesting music. There are ways to make lots more different notes on a stringed instrument.

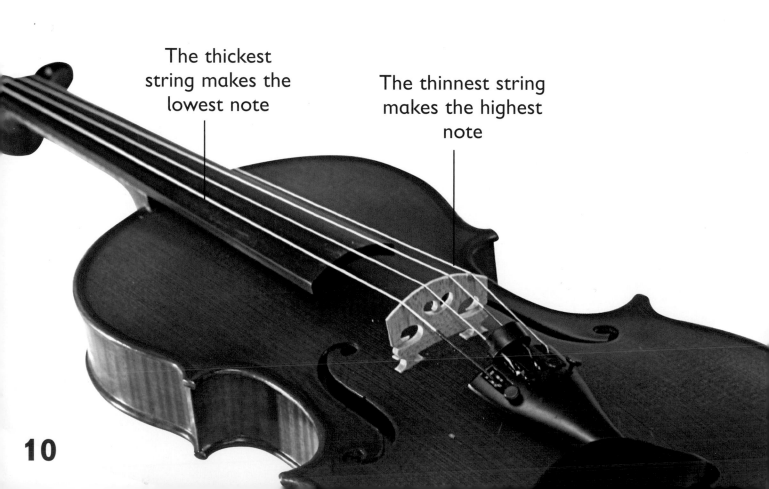

The thickest string makes the lowest note

The thinnest string makes the highest note

High and low

Some musical notes are high and some are low. We call this their **pitch**.

If you make a string shorter, it will make a higher note. You can do this by pressing your finger on it.

Another way to make a higher note is to make the string tighter.

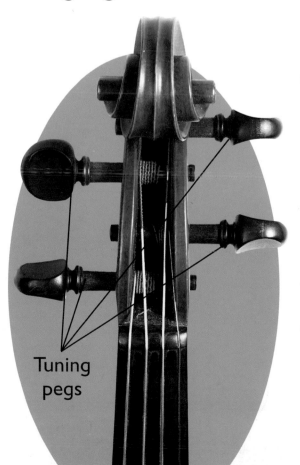

Tuning
pegs

Tuning

Before you start to play, you must check that each string plays the correct note. This is called tuning.

You tune a violin by turning the tuning pegs.

11

Playing notes

If you press the bow hard on the strings, the sound will be loud. If you press gently, the sound will be quieter.

Playing pizzicato

Sometimes you play a violin by plucking the strings with your fingers. This is called '**pizzicato**'. It sounds very different to when you use a bow.

Playing a violin pizzicato.

Long and short

To play a note that lasts a long time, use the whole length of the bow. For a short note, take the bow off the string quickly.

Music notes

To be able to play music that other people have made up, or composed, you need to understand how to read music.

Music is written in musical notes. There are **symbols** to tell us how long or short a note is. The length of the notes make up the **rhythm** of a piece of music.

The notes are written on five lines called a stave. The place of a note on the stave tells us how high or low it is. This is called its pitch.

| A long note | A short note | A low note | A high note |

This girl is playing a long note.

13

Different sizes

Here are more stringed instruments that are played with a bow. The bigger the instrument is, the deeper the sound it makes.

The violin and viola

A violin has a high pitch. A viola is bigger than a violin and has a lower pitch. These instruments can be played standing up or sitting down. They are held under the chin.

Violin.

Viola.

The cello

This is much bigger than a viola and has a deeper pitch. The player sits down to play it and holds it between her knees.

Double bass.

Cello.

The double bass

This is the largest stringed instrument played with a bow. It has a very low pitch. The player sits on a high stool and rests the double bass between his knees.

The guitar

A guitar is a stringed instrument too. To make music with it, you strum the strings with your fingers or pluck them with a piece of plastic called a plectrum.

Playing a guitar with a plectrum.

Plectrums come in different colours and patterns.

Strumming a guitar.

How to play

To hold a guitar, put it under one arm and support the neck with your other hand. To play notes, hold down the strings on the fingerboard in different places.

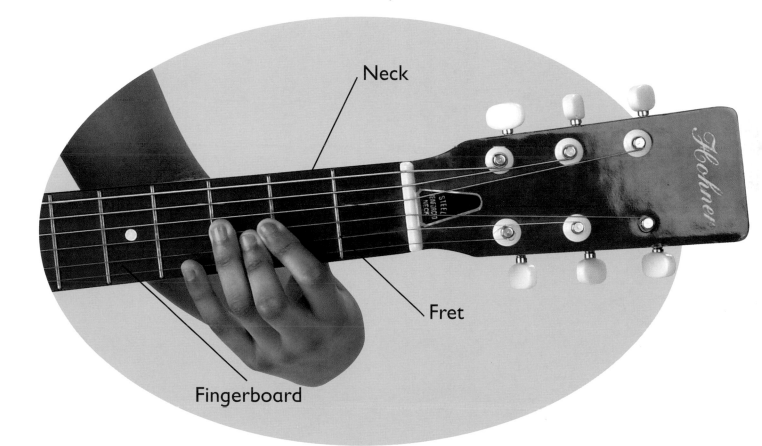

Neck

Fret

Fingerboard

The fingerboard has pieces of metal on it that mark it into sections. These are called frets. The frets help to show you where to put your fingers to change the notes.

Acoustic guitar

There are two kinds of guitar – acoustic and electric.

An **acoustic** guitar has a hollow body, which makes the sound louder in the same way as a violin (see page 9). It is made of wood.

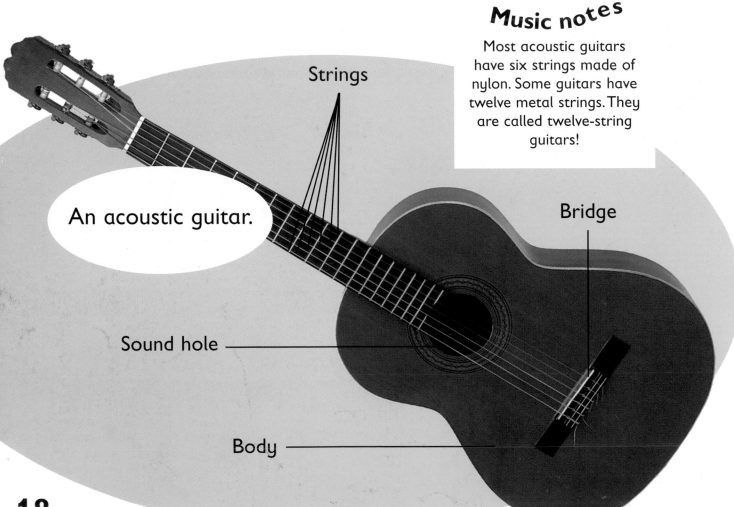

Strings

An acoustic guitar.

Sound hole

Body

Bridge

Music notes

Most acoustic guitars have six strings made of nylon. Some guitars have twelve metal strings. They are called twelve-string guitars!

Spanish guitar

The acoustic guitar is sometimes called the Spanish guitar because it is used to play Spanish music called flamenco.

Stamp your feet

There are special dances for flamenco music. Flamenco dancers stamp their feet and clap their hands as part of the dance.

A flamenco dancer.

Playing flamenco music.

Electric guitar

An electric guitar has metal strings and is made of solid wood. It needs electricity to make it work.

Strings

Most electric guitars have six metal strings.

Electric bass guitars have four strings and a very low pitch.

An electric guitar.

Strings

Pick-ups

Controls for changing **volume** and **tone**

Lead that plugs into the **amplifier**

Loud noise

An electric guitar has 'pick-ups' under the strings.

The pick-ups turn the vibrations from the strings into sound by using an amplifier that stands on the floor. The sound comes out through a **loudspeaker**.

Rock and pop music

Electric guitars are popular with pop and rock groups. They usually have at least one guitar and a bass guitar.

Music notes

The volume of an electric guitar can be turned up and down.
It can be made much louder than the volume of an acoustic guitar.

Lead

Small practice amplifier

Lead into electricity supply

Loudspeaker

More strings

Many different types of stringed instruments are played in countries all over the world. Here are just a few of them.

Kora
The kora comes from West Africa. It is made from the hollowed-out shell of a fruit called a gourd.

Sitar
The sitar comes from South Asia. It has about twenty metal strings and can be over 1 m long.

Bouzouki

This instrument comes from Greece. It is played with a plectrum and has a metallic sound.

Balalaika

This instrument is from Russia. It is shaped like a triangle and comes in six different sizes. Musicians play folk music on it. There are also balalaika **orchestras**.

The orchestra

An orchestra is a large number of musicians who play together.

There are different types of orchestra. The largest is a **symphony** orchestra, which has about one hundred musicians.

Stringed instruments make up over half of a symphony orchesta.

Can you name the stringed instruments in this orchestra?

The harp

A harp is sometimes part of the string section of an orchestra. It stands on the floor and you play it by plucking the strings with your fingers.

A harp has forty-seven strings.

Playing together

Smaller groups of musicians also play together. This group of four people has two violins, a viola and a cello. It is called a string quartet.

A string quartet.

Express yourself

There is much more to music than just playing notes. Stringed instruments can sound very different if they are played in different ways.

Feelings

Music can cheer you up, make you relax or even feel sad. It might be very loud and exciting, or quiet and peaceful.

This guitarist is playing loud rock music.

This guitarist is playing a bass guitar in a **jazz** band.

Music notes

The speed at which a piece of music is played is called its **tempo**.

Listen!

Websites

Stringed instruments

See and hear the family of stringed instruments at:
http://ngfl.northumberland.gov.uk/music/orchestra/string.htm

Explore the orchestra with the New York Philharmonic at:
www.nyphilkids.org
Walk through the instrument storage room to find out about the stringed instruments, then play Instrument Frenzy to sort out the instruments before a concert.

Click on the string section of the orchestra to listen to each instrument, including the harp, at the children's website of the San Francisco Symphony Orchestra:
www.sfskids.org/templates/instorchframe.asp?pageid=3

Guitar

See video of flamenco guitarists, including Juan Diego, at:
www.flamenco-world.com/video/videos_guitar.htm

Read an interview with a jazz guitarist (who started playing when he was six years old) and listen to his music at:
www.jazzguitar.be/jazz_guitar_free_mp3_chris_standring.html

Sitar

Watch video of Anoushka Shankar, daughter of the world-famous sitar player, Ravi Shankar, at:
www.anoushkashankar.com

Listen to more sitar music at:
www.biswabratachakrabarti.com/english/audio/audio.html

Kora

Hear Mamadou Diabate, the famous kora player from Mali in West Africa, at: *www.mamadoukora.com/recordings.html*

See photos of koras being made at a Gambian kora workshop at: *www.coraconnection.com/flash/index.html*

Visit Sound Junction, at the Associated Board of the Royal Schools of Music, to learn more about the kora and hear kora music at: *www.soundjunction.org/Allaboutthekora.aspa*

Balalaika

See photos, watch video and download mp3 files of balalaika music at: *www.barynya.com/balalaika.htm*

Bouzouki

Watch videos of different bouzouki players at: *www.mpouzouki.com*

CDs

Listen to these well-known pieces of orchestral music to hear the strings:

Elgar: *Serenade for Strings* – 'Introduction and Allegro'.
Britten: *Simple Symphony*.
Saint-Saëns: *Danse Macabre* (violin). *Carnival of the Animals* –
  'The Swan' (cello); 'The Elephant' (double bass).
Tchaikovsky: *Swan Lake* – 'Swans' (no. 13) (violins). *Nutcracker* –
  'Waltz of the Flowers' (harp).
Vaughan Williams: *Lark Ascending* (violin).

Listen to these examples of bouzouki music:

Iordanis Tsomidis: *The Music of Greece*.
Michalis Terzis: *Magic of the Greek Bouzouki*.

Glossary

Acoustic Describes an instrument that does not use electricity to produce sound.

Amplifier A piece of equipment for increasing the strength of a sound.

Jazz A style of music that began in New Orleans, USA, around the beginning of the twentieth century.

Loudspeaker A device for changing electrical signals into sounds that we can hear.

Orchestra A large group of performers playing various musical instruments.

Pitch A high musical note or sound is said to have a high pitch. A low musical note or sound is said to have a low pitch.

Pizzicato A way of playing strings by plucking them with the fingers instead of using a bow.

Rhythm The regular pattern of sound in music.

Sound wave A wave that transmits sound through the air.

Strumming Playing a stringed instrument by running your fingers lightly across the strings.

Symbol A shape or image used to represent something else.

Symphony A long piece of instrumental music written for a big orchestra.

Tempo The speed at which music is played.

Tone The quality of a sound. For example, it could be sharp or soft.

Vibrates; vibration Moving backwards and forwards, or up and down, very quickly.

Volume The strength of a sound: it can be loud or quiet.

Index